# LAS VEGAS, NEW MEXICO

Las Vegas Train Station

# LAS VEGAS, NEW MEXICO

## *A Portrait*

PHOTOGRAPHS BY
Alex Traube

WITH A TEXT BY
E. A. Mares

THE UNIVERSITY OF NEW MEXICO PRESS • ALBUQUERQUE

Library of Congress Cataloging in Publication Data

Traube, Alex, 1946–
    Las Vegas, New Mexico.

    1. Las Vegas (N.M.)—Description and travel—Views.
2. Las Vegas (N.M.)—History.    I. Mares, E. A., 1938–
II. Title.
F804.L3T7   1983          978.9′55              83–10179
ISBN 0-8263-0670-5

Manufactured in the United States of America.
International Standard Book Number 0-8263-0670-5.
Library of Congress Catalog Card Number 83-10179.
*First Edition.*

THE ESSAY THAT ACCOMPANIES this book is intended as a docu-drama, using the written word as one form of imaginative resonance to the photographs. It is not a work of original historical research. This essay would not have been possible, however, without the work of other writers and historians on Las Vegas. A special debt of gratitude is owed to Lynn Perrigo, whose *Gateway to Glorieta: A History of Las Vegas, New Mexico* is the only serious major historical work on Las Vegas and its environs. Dr. Perrigo's work is fundamental to an understanding of Las Vegas.

Other valuable works consulted are too numerous to list, but a few of the most useful were: Ellen Threinenn's *Architecture and Preservation in Las Vegas: A Study of Six Districts* (Las Vegas, 1977), "The Montezuma Hotel," in *New Mexico Architecture Magazine* (May–June 1977), Milton C. Nahm's *Las Vegas and Uncle Joe: the New Mexico I Remember* (University of Oklahoma Press, 1964), Josiah Gregg's *The Commerce of the Prairies* (University of Nebraska Press, 1967), Marcus Whiffen's *American Architecture Since 1780* (MIT Press, 1981), David J. Weber's *Foreigners in Their Native Land: Historical Roots of the Mexican Americans* (University of New Mexico Press, 1973, 1981), Erna Fergusson's *New Mexico: A Pageant of Three Peoples* (University of New Mexico Press, 1951, 1980), Marc Simmons's *New Mexico* (W. W. Norton, 1977). Also useful was *Entre Verde y Seco* by Estevan Arellano et al. (Academia Publications, 1972).

Many individuals made valuable contributions in conversations about Las Vegas. Foremost were Diana and Joe Stein of Los Artesanos Bookstore in Las Vegas, John and Margaret Geffroy, Facundo Valdez, Tomás Atencio, and Patricia Clark Smith.

*Albuquerque, New Mexico*

E. A. MARES

This book is dedicated to Reg Loving, whose friendship, encouragement, and love of New Mexico have enriched my life and have altered its course more than once.

A. T.

A PROJECT SUCH AS THIS cannot be accomplished without the support of many generous and usually anonymous individuals, some of whom I would like to thank here. First, I would like to thank Joe and Diana Stein, of Los Artesanos Bookstore, in Las Vegas, who have been good friends and who put me in touch with Tony Mares. Richard Rudisill and Arthur Olivas, both of the Historical Wing of the Museum of New Mexico, Santa Fe, have been key figures in this book finding its way into print. Carmen Holguin, Dan Holguin, Silas Lopez, and Melissa Bartlett each gave me the support and friendship necessary to make my two-year stay in Las Vegas a pleasure. Thanks to Michael Tincher of Santa Fe for helping me work out the technical problems involved in printing negatives from the Widelux Camera used in this project. Thanks to my friend John Beckman for originally putting the camera in my hands. And many thanks to Steve Catron for his inestimable help in preparing the prints for reproduction.

The work for this book was completed during the time I was working as a resident artist in the New Mexico Artist-in-the-Schools Program in Las Vegas. I wish to thank the New Mexico Arts Division for the opportunity. Particularly, I would like to thank Richard L. Cook, Diana Fish, and Michael Jenkinson. Finally, I would like to thank the University of New Mexico Press, whose faith in my work and whose willingness to produce a book of high quality has been a fine and rare experience.

All photographs in this book were taken with a Widelux Camera. The lens on this camera moves when the shutter is released and takes in a 170-degree angle of vision, or, approximately what our eyes see. It was my intention to have the work look like a walk through the city of Las Vegas, for which the Widelux seemed the perfect tool. The photographs in this book were made in the winter and spring of 1982, with the exception of the opening parade sequence, which was made in the late fall of 1981.

*Santa Fe, New Mexico*

ALEX TRAUBE

IT ALWAYS RAINS ON THE PARADE. The wet streets cast up a blurred, ghostlike world as if this moment caught by the camera conjures up all the generations that have lived, or may yet come to live, in this small town at the foot of the mountains, on the edge of the plains. A parade is a symbol of birth, of renewal, of the life-giving forces that dwell in the streets, alleys, buildings, and neighborhoods of a town or city.

At first glance, this could be a parade in any small town in the United States. There are reminders everywhere that this is Main Street, U.S.A. The Pepsi sign above the Spic and Span Cafe is familiar. Brooke Shields is playing in *Endless Love* at the Serf. The pom-pom girls and the high school band appear as they do in thousands of similar parades across the country. The flags, uniforms, and mounted posse are familiar ingredients for this kind of event. The appearance is deceptive, however, for this small town is Las Vegas, New Mexico.

The rain puddles on Douglas Avenue reflect back a variety of faces not found in an ordinary American small town. Hispanic faces. Mexican faces. Indian faces. A scattering of Anglo faces and perhaps one black face in the crowd. The figures in heavy clown makeup stare into the eye of the camera that is staring at them with the full weight and intensity of one moment snatched, however temporarily, from the consummate oblivion of time. Here is birth, the theater of ongoing life, the passing parade presided over by the Incredible Hulk, a fantasy figure from one culture who passes over the masked figures from another culture. Behind the masks and the fantasies, a whole history of masked figures and phantasmagoric characters have come onto this stage to act out their one encounter between life and death in these meadows, *las vegas*, at the foot of the Sangre de Cristo mountains.

Las Vegas, New Mexico, is a collective fact of geography, history, and passion. Many of the elements that have gone into the making of the United States, particularly the Southwest, have been caught and held here, as it were, by countervailing forces. Sedentary Pueblo Indian and raiding Comanche. Mexican rancher and German-Jewish merchant. Gunslinger and lawman. Luxury hotels and generational poverty. Economic boom and bust. A brief, passing splendor and the long backslide into the rural backwaters of the American Southwest. The classic columns of the Bank of Las Vegas are meant to indicate, ultimately, the strength and solidity of American culture and its identification with the larger frame of reference, Western Civilization and its ancestry rooted in Greece and Rome. The girls sitting on the hoods of late model cars, on the other hand, show a more recent tradition, rooted in Hollywood and the film goddesses, the beauty queens who inhabit our advertising and our dreams.

A comparison, extravagant perhaps but interesting, might be made between Las Vegas and Vienna. As Vienna was once the capital of the vast Hapsburg Empire, so Las Vegas, on a much smaller scale, was once the economic capital of a huge rural hinterland. In its prime, about a century ago, Las Vegas was the center of the cattle and sheep industry in New Mexico. It conducted a lively trade in wool, hides, and grain. The merchants of the town built splendid buildings and fostered the arts and cultural life. Despite the shortage of water, promising attempts were made to establish productive industries. As Vienna lost its eminence with the disintegration of the Hapsburg Empire, so Las Vegas, again on a smaller scale, saw its commercial empire melt away to the new centers of Denver, in the north, Albuquerque and El Paso in the south and west, and Phoenix even farther west. As Vienna was a meeting place for an immense variety of Western and Eastern peoples, so Las Vegas was the common ground for a complex mixture of sedentary and nomadic Native Americans, lumped together as "Indians," a kaleidoscope of Spanish-speaking people lumped together as "Mexicanos," "Hispanos," "Chicanos," or "Spanish Americans," depending on the political, sociological, or ideological bent of the person doing the categorizing, and that welter of immigrants and sons of immigrants who are collectively referred to as either "gringos," in moments of humor or anger, or "Anglos" when a more neutral term is sought.

The mountainous and Hispanic heartland of New Mexico juts down like an ancient flint arrowhead, with the tip resting on Albuquerque. The western edge of the arrowhead runs on a line of rugged country northwest of Chama. Its base continues east to Raton. The eastern edge slants down through Las Vegas. This is the most dramatic part of the arrowhead, for it very roughly follows a line dividing mountains from prairie, the Pueblo Indians from nomadic Apaches and Comanches, and Hispanic ranchers and small farmers from Anglo cattlemen and businessmen.

Originally, the land was Indian. Cutting its way through the Rocky Mountains, the Rio Grande shaped the native life patterns for untold millenia. Following the slope of the land, this river, sacred to the Indians and to all who know the value of water in the Southwest, drops down to the desert regions of the southern part of the state, the country the Spaniards called "la jornada del muerto," or "the dead man's journey," so forbidding was the appearance and the reality of this region.

Even when the day is cloudy, as on the day of the high school homecoming parade in Las Vegas, there is a peculiar quality of light in New Mexico. The luminosity of the sun on the harsh edges of the mountains and the semiarid tablelands seems to call into doubt the very solidity of matter. Mountain and prairie, flint edge of sunlight and shadow, a line dividing two cultures, two traditions, two currents of people, one Indohispanic and the other Anglo, focal point for the high school homecoming parade and for the historic forces that meet in its streets; this is Las Vegas, New Mexico.

II

Las Vegas began, not as a town, but as an appealing river crossing, a valley of pleasant meadows through which flowed the Gallinas River. For thousands of years before the founding of the town, these meadows were directly in the path of historic migrations and later trade routes. The high tablelands to the east, known as the Las Vegas Plateau, slope down into the valley of the Gallinas. Southwest of the Gallinas, there is a low range of hills that opens to the valley of a much larger river, the Pecos. Long before this opening was named Kearney's Gap, in honor of General Stephen Watts Kearney, United States Army, who occupied the Hispanic Southwest on behalf of the expansionist North American nation in 1846, nomadic and Pueblo Indians had used it to move back and forth from the open plains to the mountainous country. North of the Pecos River, the Sangre de Cristos rise steeply, while to the south a long rambling plateau, Glorieta (Rowe) Mesa, angles to the south and west. Continuing south, the land narrows to Glorieta Pass and Apache Canyon. Beyond to the south and west is the watershed of the Rio Grande and the pathway to Mexico.

These deceptively peaceful green meadows on the Gallinas River, in reality a gentle stream most of the year, formed one link, but a critical one, between the great plains of North America and the valley of the Rio Grande that pointed the way, in turn, south to Chihuahua and Mexico City. The colonizing Spaniards used this natural pathway and spread their pattern of settlement north from Mexico City to Santa Fe, along what came to be known as the Chihuahua Trail. By the early nineteenth century, Anglo-American traders and merchants were moving in the opposite direction, heading south and west on what they called the Santa Fe Trail. In reality, the two trails were one pathway between different cultures.

Despite the ideal geographic location for a settlement, Las Vegas was the last major Hispanic town to be established in northern New Mexico. The reasons for this are not

difficult to understand. Once the Apache and Comanche had acquired the horse, there was no adequate defense against them available to either the Indo-Hispano settler, the Pueblo Indian, or the Anglo pioneer. The raids were utterly devastating for all settlers in the area. The early nineteenth century could only be described as a nightmarish experience for Pueblo Indians or Indo-Hispanos alike who ventured very far east of Glorieta Pass. For ten years, Don Luis C. de Baca tried to maintain his land grant along the meadows of the Gallinas River. By 1831, he had to withdraw from his lands because of severe livestock losses to marauding Apaches and Comanches. Within a few years, the last seventeen survivors of Pecos Pueblo gave up the ghost and abandoned the site in order to join their relatives in the safer confines of Jemez Pueblo to the west and much farther away from the menacing great plains.

The meadows remained attractive, despite everything, and the sheer pressure of Hispanic population growth in the narrow Pecos valley began to exert a new force for a settlement along the banks of the Gallinas. After 1821, San Miguel del Bado had become a thriving town on the Santa Fe Trail, not far from the Pecos Pueblo. The cramped geography made the meadows and the open spaces to the east very appealing, although the Indian pressure continued. Early in 1835, Juan de Dios Maese, Miguel Archuleta, Manuel Duran, and Jose Antonio Casaus received from the Mexican government authorities a Las Vegas land grant officially entitling them to settle the meadows along the banks of the Gallinas River. On April 6, 1835, the town was named Nuestra Senora de Los Dolores de Las Vegas, and the thirty-seven original colonists took possession of small plots of land for houses around the plaza. Each settler had access to water from the Gallinas and from the network of ditches that soon developed around the plaza. Each had access, also, to the common lands, pastures, and forests a short distance away from the plaza. The original settlers were soon joined by 127 other colonists, and Las Vegas became firmly established as an outpost of the young Mexican nation.

Today, the plaza still has something of the rugged and barren frontier appearance about it. The Victorian-vintage buildings that surround the plaza look like relics from some bygone era. The collective efforts of many generations of Las Vegans have not been able to keep a secure grasp on this small intersection between mountain and prairie, sky and earth, and the passions of differing cultures, as if nature and history here persisted and intruded into the present, massive and imperturbable as geologic strata. The antiquated Coast Guard artillery piece faces towards the Pacific Ocean some nine hundred miles away. Immediately behind the artillery piece, on the north side of the plaza, stand the one-story Dice Apartments where General Kearny addressed his newly acquired citizens from the rooftop. The little plaza, laid out according to the rules and regulations of Imperial Spain and the Republic of Mexico, still bears, nevertheless, a fair resemblance to what

the first settlers and their newly elected alcalde, or mayor, Juan De Dios Maese, saw in 1835. The land rises dramatically in the west to culminate in the towering mountains. There is the broad and barren expanse of prairie to the east. By 1821, the Conestoga wagons were rolling over those prairie lands bringing in finished products and manufactured goods along the Santa Fe Trail. Soon the wagons were lined up around the plaza of the old town of Las Vegas.

The contrast of late-nineteenth-century Victorian buildings grouped around a rural Hispanic plaza recalls an entire history of contrasts between the Indo-hispanic and the Anglo-American cultures. Spanish, and later Mexican, expansion north of Mexico City was a controlled process. Military expeditions advanced the frontier hundreds of miles north to the Rio Grande in the sixteenth century in order to cut off a feared English advance along a mythic waterway across the North American land mass. Colonizing expeditions financed by wealthy dons followed in their wake. Spanish military and ecclesiastical officials kept a close watch on each other, and towns were carefully laid out according to the traditional plan of the Spanish plaza.

Anglo-American expansion on the North American continent was a relatively uncontrolled process. Individuals and their families made decisions to move west, where seemingly unlimited land and opportunities were supposed to be available. These early pioneers followed in the wake of fur traders and trappers, the "mountainmen," sometimes French and sometimes Anglo, who blazed trails and later served as scouts and guides for the settlers and for the United States Army. The role of the army was primarily to suppress the nomadic Indians and to protect the supply lines in the westward expansion. There was no official ecclesiastical function nor was there a state-established church. The Anglo-American town developed where it appeared logical for a town to develop—at a river crossing or confluence or at a convenient point along a trade route. The American town had a haphazard appearance. It was generally based, not on a pre-planned square or plaza, but simply on two intersecting lines that stretched to infinity.

Throughout the eighteenth century and into the early nineteenth century, a thin stream of Hispanic settlers moved up the valleys and the tributaries of the Rio Grande, the Chama, and finally the Pecos River. They became the majority population in the midst of the Pueblo Indians and for the most part lived in small villages and ranches near the Pueblos. Some intermarriage occurred, and more important, a sharing of the same environment led to a more or less continual flow of information across the Indian and Hispanic cultural frontiers. The Hispanos and the Pueblos found a common bond in the land, in similar agricultural concerns, and in the Spanish language.

Imperceptibly, the Hispanos and the Pueblos drew closer together. Hispanos would consult the Indians about weather patterns, about rain, and about crops. They would listen to the medicine man with great respect. The Indians, on the other hand, would attend the Spanish Catholic Mass on Sunday and pray to the Christian God. Later, of course, they would perform their own time-honored rituals and practice their ancient beliefs.

Life was far from idyllic, but in this remote part of the Spanish Empire, there was a kind of social shelter for the evolution of distinct forms of communal sharing between peoples of different cultures. The Hispanos and the Pueblos also had a powerful common need that bound them together—the need for protection. They were hemmed in by the raids of the nomadic plains Indians, the Apache, the Comanche, and also the Navajo, who attacked from all directions.

Juan de Dios Maese, the first alcalde of Las Vegas, presided over the early growth of the town centered on the plaza. By 1846, 6,000 acres of land had been distributed as small homesteads to the settlers. By 1850, the population had risen to 1,550 persons. Isolated by the Indian raids, hemmed in by the harsh winters and by the distance through rough country from Santa Fe, seventy miles away, the Las Vegans saw their little plaza flourish despite all difficulties. It became an important trade center for two types of commerce, one of which was more or less predictable on an advancing frontier and another that was highly unusual and adventurous.

Between 1835 and 1846, the Santa Fe Trail became a booming commercial reality for Las Vegas as well as a permanent fixture in the mythology of the American West. After gaining its independence from Spain, Mexico abandoned a protectionist economic policy and in 1821 opened up its most northerly frontier for trade with the United States. Many Mexican voices were raised in protest against the naiveté of this policy which, in effect, invited a powerful nation and potential adversary to cross at will into Mexican territory. The warnings went unheeded, and the Las Vegans witnessed the transformation of their home within a few short years from a small farm town into a bustling commercial center with the horses, oxen, and wagons of the merchant traders drawn up all around the plaza. Manufactured goods and supplies of all kinds were brought along the Santa Fe Trail to Las Vegas and on to other parts west and south—Santa Fe, Albuquerque, El Paso del Norte, Chihuahua, and Mexico City. These goods were exchanged for raw materials, wool, animal hides, sheep, minerals, and New Mexico village handcrafted arts. Las Vegas became a thriving focal point for much of this trade. While the Santa Fe Trail had started as a midwestern commercial venture, it also quickly became a thriving enterprise of Las Vegas.

Another kind of trade developed out of Las Vegas. It was profitable and dangerous. It was a trade conducted on the high plains between Hispanic traders and the Comanches. These traders, or comancheros, as they were known, became a part of American folklore about the Southwest. They traded cloth and trinkets for horses, mules, and buffalo hides. Eventually, the trade died out because of the extinction of the buffalo and the suppression of the Comanches by the U.S. Cavalry.

While commerce was thriving and the Las Vegas plaza was undergoing a transformation from a rural village to an important business center, the Mexican government was far away and immersed in internal difficulties. Between 1835 and 1846, the Mexican archives contain virtually no correspondence concerning Las Vegas. There was, nevertheless, a sense of loyalty on the part of Las Vegans toward Mexico. In 1837, Governor Manuel Armijo rode out of Santa Fe to suppress a popular uprising in the north. Las Vegas volunteers joined his army. In 1841, Las Vegans reacted with hostility toward a Texan attempt to take over New Mexico. They burned proclamations issued by the president of the Republic of Texas and welcomed Governor Armijo, who promptly trounced the Texans.

It was one thing to defeat a band of disorganized Texans. It was quite another matter

to have to confront the full force of an expansionist United States. Driven by a belief that it was entitled by God to expand to its "natural boundaries"—the doctrine known as Manifest Destiny—the United States declared war on Mexico in 1846 and sent invading armies, which rapidly turned the northern Mexican provinces into the American Southwest. The Army of the West under the command of General Kearney arrived at Las Vegas in August 1846. The last Hispanic town to be organized on the northern frontier under Mexican rule became
the first significant fruit of conquest for the invading U.S. Army.

No strangers to Anglo-Americans, the Las Vegans greeted General Kearney with a mixture of curiosity and caution. Many years after the event, a woman recalled a morning when, as a child, she saw tents and cannon on the hill overlooking the plaza. The hill would later be the site of New Mexico Highlands University. Most of the women and girls that day were sent off to hide on a nearby heavily forested ridge. About 150 Hispanos gathered in the plaza on the morning of August 14, 1846, to listen to their new ruler. General Kearney met with Juan de Dios Maese and then turned to the small crowd and addressed them from the low roof of the Dice Apartments. The view he had was at least similar to the view from the same spot today. There were no automobiles or imposing buildings at that time, but the plaza must have looked barren with the same absence of people that one notices today. Off on the side streets leading to the plaza were low-slung adobe houses, some with portales, or verandas, that ran the length of the home. Today, the row of adobe houses on South Pacific Avenue recalls that earlier time. Similar houses, then and now, could be found throughout the Southwest and down into northern Mexico. They are cool in summer and easy to keep warm in winter. Later generations of Americans would find these structures picturesque, charming, and romantic. According to the accounts of some of the early traders and the soldiers in Kearney's army, however, these earthen buildings were regarded as miserable mud hovels.

General Kearney held out both the carrot and the stick to the newly conquered Mexicanos. "We come among you as friends, not as enemies; as protectors, not as conquerors," he assured his audience. For those who did not resist, he promised that "not a pepper, not an onion, shall be disturbed or taken by my troops without pay or by the consent of the owner." He followed these soothing words with some advice: "He who promises to be quiet and is found in arms against me, I shall hang."

These words proved to be prophetic for years to come. Both prosperity and violence were in store for the little plaza during the next few decades. Prosperity came in the form of vastly increased trade and building activity. Violence came with the invading Anglo-American armies and with Hispanic insurgency against the invaders. Violence rode into Las Vegas in the form of gunslingers, outlaws, and the scattering of desperados, as they were called. These uprooted men roamed the West in the social chaos that ensued after the American Civil War. Violence accompanied the vigilantes, who predictably rose to meet the challenge of the outlaws.

Violence also appeared in the tragic, uncertain, and confused attempts to apply an entirely different legal system to the native inhabitants of the Southwest. One event from those early days has a haunting echo for our current concerns about sexual discrimination. A certain woman of Las Vegas, Paula Angel, resisted the advances of her brother-in-law. When he persisted, she stabbed him with a butcher knife, and the man died. Paula Angel was tried for murder, found guilty, and sentenced to be hanged by the neck until dead. A rope was flung over a convenient limb and attached to Paula's neck. She was seated in a buckboard, and at the command of the sheriff, a team of horses pulled the wagon out from under her. The sheriff, however, had neglected to tie her hands, and she grabbed the rope above her head and pulled herself up in order to thwart the hanging. The sheriff, who was Hispanic and anxious to complete his duties under the new laws, seized Paula by her legs and by pulling her down with all his weight tried to complete the hanging. At this point, the gathered crowd, also mostly Hispanic, became outraged with the sheriff's behavior and physically forced him to desist, arguing that she had now been hanged and should be released. A local Anglo judge pointed out, however, that the law stated that she must be hanged by the neck until dead. Paula Angel was promptly hanged again.

> *Paula Angel is a moaning wind*
> *through the streets of Las Vegas.*
> *Her long hair fills the mouths*
> *of drunks who fight in the bars.*
> *Her fingernails are the sharp knives*
> *that flash in the streets of Las Vegas.*
> *When the rafters of old Victorian homes*

> *groan in the Las Vegas night*
> *heavy with the weight of time,*
> *it is Paula Angel, pulling,*
> *pulling herself up*
> *by the rope around her neck.*

From the earliest days as a Mexican port of entry along the Santa Fe Trail, Las Vegas did not make a very good impression on the traders and merchants. One of the earliest of them, Josiah Gregg, passed through the area in 1832, three years before the founding of the town, and made the following observation: "At Gallinas creek we found a large flock of sheep grazing upon the adjacent plain, while a little hovel at the foot of the cliff showed it to be a rancho."

The "little hovel" grew rapidly, however, after the U.S. Army swept on to the Pacific. In the aftermath of the Mexican defeat, the commercial values and technology of the English-speaking nation greatly accelerated the development of Las Vegas. An ever-increasing number of German-Jewish merchants arrived, and before the end of the century, they had altered the appearance of the plaza into the peculiar combination of Hispanic Territorial and Victorian architecture that it is today.

During the Mexican period, Levi Keithly, a rancher and merchant, was admitted as a "foreigner" to Las Vegas. With the change in government, he would become the first local postmaster and a representative in the state legislature. After 1846, a number of newcomers arrived, who would later become prominent in the local economy and in the social and political life of the territory. Among them were John and Andres Dold, Frank Kihlberg, Michel De Marais, Pierre (Pedro) Lesperance, Emmanuel and Joseph Rosenwald, Charles Blanchard, and Charles Ilfeld. They arrived with their families, beginning in 1850, and by 1870, they had succeeded in giving the plaza substantially the characteristics it still has.

Frank Kihlberg began his business on the Santa Fe Trail. He lived in the Dice Apartments, then known as the Plaza Apartments. As seen across the plaza square and beyond the Coast Guard artillery piece, these apartments now have a modern facade. But it is not difficult to imagine them as they were and to see Mr. Kihlberg striding toward Hot Springs Avenue at the northwest corner of the plaza. On his way, he might come upon Charles Ilfeld and stop and have a chat with him.

Charles Ilfeld had been an extremely busy merchant from the time of his arrival in Las Vegas in 1865. Starting with a five-thousand-dollar loan from Don Jose Albino Baca, a wealthy Mexicano from an earlier period, Charles Ilfeld developed the leading business in New Mexico within two decades. He supplied hay and grains to army forts, particularly Fort Union north of Las Vegas, and to the Barlow and Sanderson stagecoach lines. He provided storage facilities for the stagecoach business and held the contracts for the supplying of railroad ties to the Atchison Topeka & Santa Fe Railroad. His Las Vegas store serviced a trade area that extended north to the Colorado line, east into Texas, south to Roswell and Carlsbad, and west into the Sangre de Cristo mountain villages.

Prosperity was such that by 1880, the plaza businessmen formed an association to build one of the finest hotels in the West. By late 1881, the hotel was completed. Located on the north side of the square, the hotel, called the Plaza Hotel, looks impressive over a century later. Its open-topped Baroque pediment above the triangular and arched pediment moldings of the floors below add a touch of Victorian elegance to the plaza. Virtually all of the buildings on the plaza date back a century or more. Disguised now as an auto supply business, the John Dold Building retains a touch of the Territorial style, which it at one time so eloquently expressed. With the arrival of the Americans, the one-story adobe buildings of Spanish Colonial origins were remodeled with glass windows, tin roofs, and machined lumber. The result was the Territorial style of basic adobe structures adorned now with pitched roofs, larger windows, and classical details in the moldings. Only the Dice Apartments on the plaza date back to the Mexican period.

With the coming of the railroad and the attendant increase in prosperity, a number of substantial buildings besides the Plaza Hotel were constructed. Facing east from the plaza, down Bridge Street, the First National Bank rises like a relic from the turn of the century. Built in the 1880s, this fine Victorian building today proclaims a prosperity that quickly faded. Across the street is the boarded-up shell of the Romero Building. To the west of the First National Bank is the Rosenwald Building, built in 1908 in the Neoclassical Revival style. Emmanuel Rosenwald was one of the merchants who helped bring prosperity to Las Vegas about a century ago. His building housed one of the major wholesale firms until the 1920s. Since then, the building has housed a parachute factory and a textile firm. Today, the boarded-up

front and the broken windows stand as sad witness to a vanished splendor.

To this day, the plaza carries with it the contrasts of its origins and development. Spanish Colonial in the beginning, the Anglo-American nation brought a Territorial overlay and the prosperity of the Victorian period. Even when the new prosperity was about to appear in the form of the railroad, there was a hint of the future decline. Eagerly anticipating the approach of the railroad, the town fathers named the narrow dirt road leading south from the plaza South Pacific Avenue, for the railroad would strike south and west from the plaza, they assumed, and continue on toward the Pacific. They were wrong. The railroad came through east of town, in 1879, and the Old Town was bypassed in favor of the new City of Las Vegas that sprang up around the railroad tracks.

To look down South Pacific Avenue today is to turn from the brief Victorian glory of the plaza back to the quieter times of the early nineteenth century. The steel-link fence is a reminder that this is the late twentieth century, as are the other artifacts of our times—the television antenna, the telephone posts, and the metal bumper fence along the shoulder of the road. Yet it is possible to ignore these signs of modernity and concentrate on the long portal with its old paint-flaked picket fence, the pickets broken and missing like teeth in the smile of an old-timer who has survived the many transformations of this western town. The Territorial-style adobe houses on Hot Springs Boulevard are also reminders of a preindustrial time.

Where the sun strikes along a south wall, or east wall in the afternoon, the Hispano old-timers would gather at the *resolana*, the place filled with sunshine. They would gossip about the day's events, about politics, and about the general drift of affairs in the lives of the villagers. Here in the sun-filled plazas and along the sun-spattered walls of the narrow, meandering dirt roads, tales of bygone days were recounted. The myths, beliefs, and historic events that had shaped the community were passed down from the elders to the younger generation. When the land was gone, jobs were scarce or nonexistent, and poverty and welfare dependency became the daily lot of thousands of Nuevo Mexicanos *norteños*, humor would more often than not come to the rescue. Humor and a gentle philosophy of life that was stoic and humane carried the Hispanos from one way of life across all the political, social, and economic pitfalls, to the new way of life that was to develop for them, for their children, and for their children's children, whose descendants today make up a substantial proportion of the New Mexican population.

Spanish sayings have captured the gentle philosophy and the humor typical of Las Vegas and other northern New Mexico communities. "Life is a door through which we all pass," one saying reminds us, "each at his own pace, looking for the best and many times encountering what we least expected." "He who feeds a stranger's dog," goes another saying, "loses his bread and also his own dog." "Don't spit at heaven," advises another saying, "for it will fall back in your face." The Hispano loss of land was preserved in memory by fables:

"Once upon a time, there was a crow with a bit of cheese in its mouth. Suddenly a fox appeared, who said to the crow that she enjoyed hearing him sing since he had such a lovely voice. Filled with pride, the crow began to sing. As soon as he opened his mouth, he dropped the cheese, and the fox scooped it up and ran away laughing at the crow."

There is a haunted and a haunting quality about Las Vegas. This is a town haunted by the Indo-Hispanic past, haunted by the Victorian moment of glory, and haunted by the challenges of the twentieth century. It is a town haunting in its harshness, its beauty, and its sadness, haunting in its disappointments and its ever-renewing hopes. Nothing signaled the challenges that lay ahead as clearly as the arrival of the Atchison, Topeka & Santa Fe Railroad in 1879.

### III

If the stranger's dog had been fed in 1846, then the fox ran away with the cheese in 1879, for in that year the railroad came to Las Vegas, and the steam engines were bellowing and belching out the loud, boisterous, and at times dark portents of the future. Nothing about the Las Vegas Railroad Station today indicates that it was once the exciting vanguard of the American railroad expansion into the Southwest. The nation was to be linked by steel rails and by the promise of unlimited economic growth. There is no sign of that excitement today. The station is small, and the tracks stretch toward the northern and southern horizons with a vacant look reminiscent of a De Chirico painting. When the 4:30 P.M. Amtrack train comes through town, it barely pauses for a few minutes to take on an occasional passenger before it goes roaring off to the south toward Albuquerque, Gallup, Flagstaff, and beyond to Los Angeles, or, at another time, if it is going in the opposite direction, to whisk away a Las Vegan toward the almost inconceivably different worlds of Chicago and New York.

Most of the railroad towns that grew up alongside the tracks in the 1870s and the 1880s had a brief boom. They developed along a main street that paralleled the railroad tracks. Eventually, the wealthier residential areas blossomed on the right side of the tracks, and the poor people remained on the wrong side of the tracks.

Where the railroad passed through or near Hispanic towns already established, a series of "New Towns" developed near the "Old Towns." Las Vegas is a good example of the Old Town/ New Town phenomenon. For Las Vegas, the Old Town was and remains by and large Hispanic. The German and Jewish merchants who had located on the Old Town plaza had become fairly Hispanicized by the early twentieth century. The New Town originated as, and remains predominantly to this day, an Anglo-American town. The Old Town was based on the traditional Spanish square. A Roman Catholic church was always nearby. The New Town grew up along the straight line of Main Street and was dominated by large commercial buildings. The Protestant churches were, for the most part, located in the New Town. The Old Town had a tendency to fade, economically speaking, and become the site of the smaller, less successful business establishments. New Town became the hub of prosperous commercial ventures. Socially, the Gallinas River became the dividing line between Old Town and the new Las Vegas that began to stretch out along the railroad line in 1879.

Ill omens for the future peace and stability of Las Vegas society began to abound with the coming of the railroad. Ugly racial views were part and parcel of the expansionist mentality of late-nineteenth-century America. As the railroad tracks pushed closer and closer to Las Vegas, agitation with racial overtones began in favor of a separate town. The editor of the Las Vegas *Optic* wrote that "East Las Vegas is an American town and will be governed by Americans only." He added that those who favored a single incorporated city were a "little off" in thinking that "the American people, full of activity and enterprise, would consent to lock arms and join destinies with the Mexican portion."

Throughout the 1880s, there were ethnic tensions, political irregularities, and legal uncertainties between West Las Vegas and East Las Vegas. During one fifteen-year period, 1888–1903, East Las Vegas had a separate "all Anglo" municipal government, while West Las Vegas continued under the laws of a county government where Hispanic influence was strong.

Complicating relations in the town were the endless disputes over land. The Mexican government, based on Spanish precedent, had continued the custom of granting land to individuals and their families and heirs, and also to communities. With the defeat of Mexico and the change in legal systems, chaos and confusion reigned in all issues dealing with land. In Las Vegas as elsewhere in New Mexico, unscrupulous attorneys frequently posed as champions of land-grant claimants in order to advance their own economic interests. The result in Las Vegas was the hardening of negative ethnic and social attitudes that continued to plague the area for years to come.

The split was finalized in 1903, when West Las Vegas officially became incorporated as a town. The political division between a West Las Vegas, predominantly Hispanic, preindustrial in its economic outlook, Catholic and communal in its values, and Spanish speaking, and an East Las Vegas, primarily non-Hispanic, commercial, Protestant and private, as opposed to communal, in its values, and English speaking, was to last until 1968.

More than industrial entrepreneurs and the commercially minded rode into Las Vegas with the construction of the railroad. In the after-math of the American Civil War, or the War Between the States, as Southerners prefer, substantial numbers of restless men and women arrived, who for whatever reasons no longer fit into any peaceful or orderly social pattern of existence. As the railroads pressed forward into the Southwest, they hired gunslingers from the ranks of these drifters in order to control the right of way against other, competing railroad companies. By the fall of 1879, the Atchison, Topeka & Santa Fe Railroad had won the race through Raton Pass and on to Las Vegas. Now the railroad didn't need the hired guns. Unemployed, and with time and energy to spare, the gunslingers rode into Las Vegas.

Prior to 1879, Las Vegas had been a relatively peaceful Hispanic town. What violence existed had been contained in the centuries-old social structures that medieval Spain had imposed throughout its imperial realm. For a very brief period, 1879–84, Las Vegas became one of the most lawless towns in the country. The list of frequently violent visitors to the city

reads like a "Who's Who" among the famed outlaws of the Old West. Billy the Kid, Doc Holliday, Dave Rudabaugh, Jesse James (a peaceful visitor), J. J. Webb, Billy Wilson, Tom Picket, and Clay Allison (also a peaceful visitor) frequented the bars and cantinas of the town, caroused with the ladies of the night, and occasionally engaged in mayhem. In the general swirl of activity related to setting up a new town, the distinction between lawman and outlaw was blurred. Some of the outlaws found occasional work as deputy sheriffs for Las Vegas.

Inevitably, the popular reaction to this state of affairs took the form of vigilantism. There was also an effort to find strong "law and order" types for the sheriff's job. The combination of these two forces turned the tide on the outlaws. Pat Garrett, a Las Vegas deputy sheriff and later resident of the town, gunned down Billy the Kid in Fort Sumner, in 1881. Many years later, long after the turn of the century, Pat Garrett was himself assassinated. The town's vigilantes made life increasingly uncomfortable for the

outlaws. The last of the big-time outlaws to ride into Las Vegas was Robert "Bob" Ford. He had earlier murdered Jesse James by shooting him in the back. Ford then left Kansas, and his reputation preceded him to Las Vegas. He tried to open a saloon in the town but he was greeted by such ridicule and so much hostility on the part of the vigilantes that he wisely decided it would be healthier to leave—which he promptly did.

The passing of the outlaws did not bring peace. An example of lawlessness had been set by the social outcasts of the nation. It was an example soon followed by Vicente Silva, a notorious home-grown New Mexican outlaw. Silva and his gang terrorized Las Vegas in the 1890s until he, in turn, was murdered by members of his own gang.

The turmoil of the times also led to the formation of a Hispano secret society, *Las Gorras Blancas* (the White Caps), who tried to protect what was left of their diminished lands from the increasing pressures of railroad expansion and encroachment by commercial and ranching interests. *Las Gorras Blancas* burned down the offending fences of the cattle barons, tore up the tracks of the Santa Fe Railroad, harassed the homesteaders, and made some attempt to link up with other forces of popular discontent, such as the segment of the labor movement led by Eugene Debs. Gradually, these disturbed times gave way to the more peaceful early decades of the twentieth century.

One thing for certain that can be gathered from the events of the 1880s and the 1890s in Las Vegas is that no "melting pot" of cultures and peoples occurred here. Las Vegan Hispanos, like the vast majority of their compatriots throughout northern New Mexico, retained their language, customs, beliefs, and social patterns. Las Vegas became, then, a city divided against itself along ethnic, class, and cultural lines. It became a city where two different historical currents met uncomfortably, and where they have been trying ever since to find a common ground. As the old feuds have died away, a

surface goodwill characterizes Las Vegas today. Beneath that surface, in addition to humanitarian stirrings, a legacy of historic issues and problems remains to be solved or overcome with the sheer weight of the passage of time.

When the 4:30 P.M. Amtrak train pauses briefly to take on passengers, the gleaming aluminum coaches proclaim that this train is a Superliner. It comes like a messenger from the frantic cities to the east and to the west. It is a reminder, a link, to a world that otherwise intrudes on Las Vegas primarily via the television set. The train departs in a hurry. It leaves behind only a great silence and a loneliness that cuts as deeply as the wind blowing off the plains to the east.

Left behind are the boxcars parked next to the train station and alongside a warehouse. A number of older houses dating back perhaps to the World War I era are visible in the background of the idle boxcars. It is as if the Superliner were not the reality, or only an insignificant part of the greater reality that remains after it has departed. That greater reality harkens back to an earlier era. The air is thick with silence, abandonment, and ghosts. The empty baggage cart at the end of the train station stands like a wood-and-iron sculpture made to commemorate an outmoded technology. Here, where there was so much life only a century ago, not even the presence of a late-model Detroit car, itself a relic, helps to dispel the sense of a forgotten time and a forsaken place.

Directly north of the forlorn railroad station is the Castaneda Hotel. A number of magnificent hotels were built during the period of the Great Boom of the 1880s. By 1882, the first Montezuma Hotel opened on the mountainous outskirts of town. The Plaza Hotel opened at the same time. The wealthy and the famous flooded to Las Vegas. The Castaneda was completed in 1899 and also became the rendezvous place for the affluent and the powerful. It was one of the favorite hotels of Teddy Roosevelt and his Roughriders. The Castaneda, a Harvey House, was built in the Mission Revival style favored by the Santa Fe Railroad and the Harvey House hotels. It is a fine and solid red-brick two-story building with an imposing facade and courtyard that faces the tracks.

Now the Castaneda is an empty husk. Weeds grow in the ruined garden of the courtyard. The silence is overwhelming inside the enormous hotel. There is dust and grime everywhere. The carpet is threadbare and torn in spots. The once-elegant rooms upstairs have a seedy appearance, and the broken plumbing and light fixtures are like last year's wreaths at the cemetery.

After the Panic of 1893, the Castaneda, as well as the other luxury hotels of the town, experienced a decline. Luxury hotels began to appear farther west, as the railroads penetrated deeply into the Southwest. Other resort areas and other centers of commerce and industry began to sap the strength and vitality of Las Vegas. As early as 1885, for example, Albuquerque, more centrally located in the state, had begun to surpass Las Vegas in the quantity of its trade.

Following the railroad line to the southern outskirts of town, there is an abandoned roundhouse. In the heyday of steam-driven engines, the roundhouse was the center of constant repair activity and bustle. The passing of the steam engine and the general decline of the railroads signaled the end of the roundhouse. The Las Vegas roundhouse completes the general impression of loneliness and abandonment that haunts the railroad part of town:

*the boxcars set on a siding*
*the rails turn into rust*
*the roundhouse south of Las Vegas*
*has weeds inside numerous as headstones*
*and it cries like an old woman to herself*
*for her dead children*
*the purpose-bound engine and the desolate*
  *whistle*

*come down the tracks remorseless as*
  *memory*
*a great blur of thunder and churning pistons*
*the ocean roar of iron wheels coming closer*
*the train circling back*
*all these nights and days*
*the train comes back*
*from childhood sleep and dreams*

IV

Interstate 25 cuts east from Santa Fe through Apache Canyon and Glorieta Pass. The highway follows Rowe Mesa in an easterly direction until it turns north again at Starvation Peak, near Bernal, and continues on through Las Vegas. It is the path of the Old Santa Fe Trail, much improved as far as roads go, and the land it traverses in north-central and northeastern New Mexico is awesome. The Sangre de Cristo Mountains, the "Blood of Christ" Mountains, come tumbling down out of Colorado to form the southernmost fastness of the Rocky

Mountains. It is the land shaped like a rough, primeval arrowhead pointing south, a land of spectacular beauty, thin soil, a short growing season, and fiercely cold winters. Oliver La Farge referred to this land as "vast, harsh, poverty-stricken, varied, . . . a breeder of artists and warriors." He saw New Mexico as "primitive, underdeveloped, overused, new, raw, rich with tradition, old, and mellow . . . a land full of the essence of peace, although its history is one of invasions and conflicts. It is itself an entity, at times infuriating, at times utterly delightful to its lovers, a land that draws and holds men and women with ties that cannot be explained or submitted to reason." The traveler heading north might swing off the interstate at Las Vegas and take old route U.S. 85 through the town. U.S. 85 bypasses West Las Vegas and its aesthetically pleasing plaza entirely as it continues past the old roundhouse parallel to Railroad Avenue, and then moves in a straight line north out of town.

The northward-bound traveler sees a typical main street of an economically depressed small American town. Here is a small cafe, there a Texaco filling station, and up ahead is a Dairy Queen drive-in. All of this is vintage 1940s or earlier. U.S. 85 is, in a sense, a mask that hides the many other faces, and other masks, of Las Vegas. By slightly changing the angle of vision of the traveler, the other faces of Las Vegas begin to reveal themselves.

One block east of U.S. 85, at the intersection of Railroad Avenue and Lincoln Street, is the Casino Bar. This intersection was the very heart of the boom-town commercial district that sprang up around Railroad Avenue a century ago. After the plaza, it was the most important commercial center until the 1893 depression sent it into decline. Looking south down Railroad Avenue from Lincoln Street, the old Atchison, Topeka & S.F. roundhouse is barely visible just below the horizon. Closer to the viewer is a line of old commercial buildings. At one end is the Ward block, a Victorian building that housed, successively, the Elks Saloon and the Golden Rule store on the first floor. The next two-story structure visible is the Isaac Lewis Building, which was a men's furnishings store and later a boardinghouse. A little closer still is the old Arcade Saloon that became the Boston Clothing House. Only the Casino Bar is of slightly more recent vintage since it was built between 1902 and 1908. A handsome building in the Baroque Revival style, it occupies the site of an earlier and very rough bar known as Ward and Tamme's Monarch Billiard Hall.

The welcoming sign on the Casino Bar refers to it as "The Fun Place." It is a local Hispano hangout. On Friday, Saturday, and Sunday, as the signs indicate, there is dancing. The music and the dancing are good in the classic northern New Mexico saloon-and-dance-hall tradition. Most of the customers are poor, and they drink in quantity the only drink they can afford—round after round of Coors or Schlitz. Between the rounds of beer, a local band, or *conjunto*, will play a variety of rock-and-roll songs, polkas, and popular Mexican corridos, the ballads that praise the deeds of heroic, comic, and tragic figures, who populate the mythological and psychological landscape of many *norteños*. The electric amplification is loud, and the beat is heavy. The dancing is continual. It is not a bad way to spend a weekend. Outside the land is flat and silent towards the east; the wind is a low note held for long durations, and the small town is a small town. Inside, however, there is a charged and intense atmosphere of goodwill, occasional anger and violence, and immense erotic vitality. The corridos recount the virtues, the vices, and the usually sad fate of romantic heroes and heroines. Many of the ballads come from the period of the Mexican revolution of 1910. The polkas, the occasional *chotis*, Scottish dances, and the contemporary rock-and-roll songs create a feeling of warmth and closeness.

The Casino Bar, like all good bars in northern New Mexico, is more than just a dispensary of the universal, all-purpose, tragicomic drug, alcohol. It is a mythic gathering place, a reenactment of cosmic creative and destructive forces, a sacramental gathering of the scattered remnants of the Hispanic peoples and the relief-seeking, fun-seeking Anglos who stumble in out of the overwhelming rejection of silence and the darkness of night. There are worse ways to spend an evening in a small town.

Around the corner from the Casino Bar on Lincoln Street is the Wells-Fargo Building. It houses a radio station now, but around 1890, the Wells-Fargo Express Company had this classical Victorian building for its local headquarters. There is no sign now indicating that the famous stagecoach company once operated from here. Surely the dust-stopped mouths of the dead Express drivers would mutter a word or two, if they could, about the sleek, shiny pickup truck with its Uniroyal Fastrak tires in front of the building.

Across the street from Wells-Fargo is another local bar hangout, the Pioneer Lounge. The faded glory of the lounge is only emphasized by the once-elegant surroundings in which it is located. The building is in the Victorian Neo-classical tradition with Corinthian pilasters and a pedimented parapet. Joined to it by a one-story building is the center block. Built in the Romanesque style, its most noticeable feature is the second-story corner tower. The Romanesque arches and the tower give the center block a distinctively medieval ambience. The broken windows add to the air of an abandoned castle.

Seen from Grand Avenue, the Masonic Building and the El Fidel Hotel continue in the Romanesque and Victorian tradition of the older Lincoln Avenue buildings. The Fidel brothers, of Syrian origin, immigrated to New Mexico in the early years of this century and built a chain of

sumptuous hotels. Old-timers, retirees from the Santa Fe Railroad, gather in the lobby to reminisce about earlier times. The bar does a lively business at night, and it is a good place for local gossip.

Whole generations have been born, grown up, and passed away in the shadows of these venerable old buildings. When the buildings were young, there was still the promise of future growth for Las Vegas. The dreams were still-born. Other better-located, more-dynamic, politically and culturally less-complicated towns developed into cities throughout the Southwest. Las Vegas was left with its structural relics from the turn of the century. They failed as harbingers of prosperity, and now they stand watch over a vanished future. There is something ghostlike about them and also about the Las Vegas landscape that they mark with their presence. Standing at attention, as if waiting to assemble for a parade that is never to occur, these Victorian period pieces imply the ultimate failure of human material ambition, the tragic

warp and woof of existence built into the time clocks of stars, galaxies, and human beings.

No matter how haunted by the forms and memories of the past, no matter how harsh the material poverty of the present, life comes bursting forth through all the interstices in the dumb walls of matter. Weeds push up around telephone poles and fire hydrants, or along the side of a building bordering on an alley, and everywhere the human presence makes itself known and leans into the future. No matter how dilapidated the commercial symbols of twentieth-century America—the shabby and faded Coca Cola sign mounted on a chipped and pitted concrete block—there is an enduring human touch. Tony's Food Market (a fine name for a down-to-earth no-nonsense source of sustenance) proclaims that here is life and that its needs will be met. No matter the signs of generational poverty along Eleventh Street, there is still the boisterousness of graffiti on the tin-sided shacks. At Jackson Avenue and Tenth Street, no matter that the pavement is badly in need of repair and the old trees have been reduced to lifeless truncated stubs of wood; the Victorian house is well maintained, the fir tree is magnificent, and the television antenna indicates that inside the walls of the house, humans are struggling, like all of their own kind, to find something to do with the onrushing moments of the future that come pressing into their lives.

There is room for humor in this landscape. The Jaycees parade car proudly displays the outline map of New Mexico on its door with the Zia sun symbol in the center. Never mind that the fenders and hood of the car are missing, for the car seems to fit even better this way into the total context of New Mexico. This is a harsh, unadorned land. The great beauty of the land here is not decorative. Rather it is the beauty of bright moonlight filtering through the ribs of a long-dead horse or cow on the high plains, stark, clean, classic. So the Jaycee car has an honest beauty that is able to laugh at itself, with an old cowboy saddle mounted on a steel barrel attached above the trunk and rear seat. Who knows what great beast might come roaring out of Las Vegas high in the saddle on the Jaycee car bound for a new Jerusalem? The view from the corner of Tenth and Jackson is a reminder that this is also a quiet midwestern kind of town, a solid last link in a social chain that stretches across the pioneer plains back to Kansas, Missouri, and Illinois. A shaded alley and a picket fence reiterate the midwestern character that is part of the complex human geography of this town.

Las Vegas struggled after the turn of the century to maintain the prosperous drive that had sustained it before. The town, or rather the two towns of East Las Vegas and West Las Vegas, never quite recovered from the Crash of 1893. Many sporadic attempts to establish local industries bore scant fruit. Something of a commercial center did grab hold on Douglas Avenue, and it remains a lively part of town to this day.

Murphy's Drugstore is a gathering place for

the junior-high and high-school set. During the sun-drenched days of July, an ice-cream cone at Murphy's adds just the right balance to the hot days of summer. Up the block from Murphy's the demolition of the Montgomery Ward Building raises questions about the stability of middle America and its values. When a building dies, it is something like a galaxy that burns up and collapses upon itself in the heavens. The life of man is brief, but buildings, even flimsy buildings, appear indestructible for years. Countless people enter through their doors, scurry around inside, and then depart. A speeded-up movie would show the bizarre, intricate, funny, and sad dance of human forms against the structures of their own creation. The buildings themselves change only imperceptibly, usually in the quiet decay that comes over many years, as with the Victorian period buildings of the town. Buildings, unlike humans, can be dramatically rescued at the last minute and given a second chance, restored to true youthfulness for many years to come,

rather than the simulacrum of face lifts, hair dyes, make-up, plastic surgery, and plastic inserts that prop up the dying flesh of our kind to make a theatrical joke on youth played out from middle age to the last days of life. Buildings aren't always rescued, however, and suddenly one of them goes down, is demolished. As it goes down, holes begin to appear in the personal histories of men, women, and children who have grown up with this building, who have had dialogue with it in the language of interacting forms, who have taken it for granted as an object among many other objects that serve as psychological mirrors for a sense of time and place in one's personal history. Suddenly the building is gone. When the high-school parade marches down this street next year, the building will be missed as a school-mate is missed who graduated last year, left town, and has not been heard from since.

The general poverty and isolation of Las Vegas has given even its contemporary appearance a period-piece quality. The industry and commerce of the last century are as remote from the present, despite the scattered Victorian sentinels, as the Comanches and Apaches who once moved throught the meadows, watered their horses, and marauded through Kearney's Gap down into the Pecos country.

The '58 Ford in front of the J. C. Penney Company on Douglas Avenue is caught in the same time warp as the rest of the town. It is at once a memory of luxury from another time and place in America and a joyful celebration of the moment. There is nothing finer than to circle the town slowly in your '58 Ford on a Saturday night, Chuck Berry coming at you from the radio, a cold six-pack on the floor board, and a good woman at your side. It is as much a thing to do as anything else while doing time on the third planet, in a remote corner of that planet, beneath the New Mexico sky that plummets right down to the ground and sweeps you back up to the stars.

A proper middle-class and middle-American mannequin stares out from the J. C. Penney store window at the corner of Sixth Street and Douglas Avenue. Or is she an apparition, a disgruntled and disembodied pioneer woman who found no fulfillment here at the end of the plains come back now in modern garb to nag the present about those hard times and her lot? The scarcity of mannequins and clothes on display is an indication of a depressed economy. Weeds attack the tiled corner of the building and the base of the wall along Eighth Street. The weeds, somehow, are not out of place or out of their own time frame and the fact that they are here is not as jarring as the presence of the J. C. Penney Building itself and the mannequins.

Several time frames confront each other at once in the photograph of the J. C. Penney store window. The mannequins of children have an Eisenhower-era bourgeois optimism about them, well groomed, stylishly dressed, and smiling contentedly, as they are, from their mindless world. Unlike the mannequins, the teddy bears are for all ages and all children. Teddy bears, when they are new, are the constant and faithful companions of infants and toddlers. Later, teddy bears become grubby and threadbare; cotton and other stuffing material begin to fall out of them; and they are shelved in dark corners of closets. They reappear at unexpected times to entertain visiting children of friends and family, or to be passed on to a younger generation, when the original owners have grown up and have children of their own. Old teddy bears show up in donation boxes as toys for the poor. Once in a while, a teddy bear may be seen in the arms of an elderly or senile person rocking back and forth in a chair against the oncoming night.

The Victorian buildings reflect back to the J. C. Penney store window their own forms from the turn of the century, the dead trees of an earlier era, and the live trees in the background. The image of the photographer himself is caught on the precipice of one moment in process toward the unknowable future. All of these images and time frames are caught by the one-eyed camera to become preserved in photo-graphs, these curious ballots by means of which we cast a tentative vote indicating our belief in some kind of a future.

When the '58 Ford cruises around the Old Town plaza, it will, in all probability, sooner or later encounter the '55 Buick parked here in front of the boarded-up Safeway Building on Douglas Avenue. The cars, unlike the manne-quins, have the warmth and charm of well-loved objects. In Las Vegas, the '55 Buick is more than mere nostalgia. It is the embodiment of the American Dream that lives on. The rakish lines with simulated portholes suggest adventure and an eye for progress toward the promising future. The white sidewall tires simulate a prosperity that was always more imagined than concrete. These classy cars from the fifties that cruise around town at low speeds on weekend nights are the dreams of the good life, the good times that never were and may never be, the dreams that will not die.

Choices are limited in a small town. One

photograph showing the city school building, the armory, the bus depot and the post office, sums it all up. Elementary and secondary education offer a hope of better jobs for some of the city's youth, further education for others, perhaps at New Mexico Highlands University right in town, or at other colleges and universities. If the educational option falters, there remain the armed services, followed by a stint in the National Guard, or the trek out of town, out of state, to search for jobs. In any case, the automobile, the train, and the Greyhound bus offer a way out for those who wish, or need, a way out of town. Inevitably, one of the links left to home will be the post office, the letters and cards at holiday times, the brief notices of births and deaths in the family, the thin lifeline of memory stretching back to the meadows and the people, the family aging here along the banks of the Gallinas.

The enduring folk who are left behind, like the elderly Hispano walking toward the store window proclaiming "Live *Free* for Life," have their memories and their dreams. There are always dreams.

V

The town of West Las Vegas and the city of East Las Vegas were actually and symbolically separated by the unimposing Gallinas River. Like so many "rivers" in the Southwest, the Gallinas is merely a small creek, at best, and usually dry enough to cross on foot without getting more than slightly damp in the process. The real separation between the two halves of the town was as wide as the separation between Spain and England and all their conflicting enterprises on the North American land mass. People of goodwill are still trying to find the common links across that chasm, the common bridge, the real Bridge Street from one culture to another.

Bridge Street, as the name implies, was intended literally to span the Gallinas River and link the Old Town around the plaza with the New Town developing around the tracks. The attempt failed, as already indicated, and the two communities remained legally separated, if not totally divorced, until the late 1960s.

Developing as it did in the railroad period, Bridge Street had, and still retains, a western "boomtown" flavor. The principal buildings are rubble stone Victorian and Period Revival. Like so many districts of Las Vegas, the Bridge Street area looks much as it did a century ago. Despite the telephone lines, light poles, and the structural repairs or modifications not in keeping with the original styles, it is not difficult to visualize Doc Holliday striding down the street or Clay Allison riding his horse slowly toward the plaza, while Pat Garrett keeps a watchful eye on him.

At the top of the hill leading toward Old Town, just before National Avenue becomes Bridge Street, is another attempt at compromise between the Hispanic and Anglo halves of Las Vegas—New Mexico Highlands University. Near the edge of the campus is a college hangout, the Campus Drive-In. It is, in many respects, like thousands of college hangouts across the nation. One glance at the menu, however, shows once again how different this town is. Alongside the usual American entrees are appetizing and delectable red and green chile burritos, menudo, posole, and enchiladas. The Marine pilot on the billboard entices the college students to leave these meadows and hills for travel and adventure.

The Ilfeld Auditorium dominates the Highlands University campus. A venerable structure completed by the Works Projects Administration during the Franklin D. Roosevelt presidency, it is the site of many of the cultural activities of the town and the university. To the left of the auditorium is a mural from the more turbulent days of the Chicano Movement at Highlands in the 1960s. Although the term *Chicano* is not well liked by

many Hispanics in northern New Mexico, it is a politically charged descriptive term that many Hispanic students readily assume.

A wind swept the United States in the 1960s. The Civil Rights movement, the anti-war movement, the student movement, embodied by such organizations as the Student Non-Violent Coordinating Committee, and the Students for a Democratic Society, challenged the smug assumptions of the Eisenhower Era. Ethnic groups across the country developed a degree of critical consciousness never before experienced on such a scale in American society. The rallying cries of "Black Power" and "Red Power" could be heard across the nation. Another term became popularized in that decade: *Chicano Power.* The term was taken up by the youngest and most activist segments of Hispanic youth in the country. Inspired by the leadership of the union organizer Cesar Chavez and by the drama, the anguished cry for social justice, and the personal courage of leaders such as Reies Lopez Tijerina, hundreds of thousands of Hispanic

youth began calling themselves "Chicanos" to distinguish themselves as activists from a mellower older generation. In Las Vegas, the militant Chicano sentiment is a reminder of the earlier *Gorras Blancas*, who tried as best they could to preserve their threatened way of life. At a much deeper level, the northern New Mexican Hispano has historically been extremely independent and hostile toward figures of governmental authority. This attitude extends far back into the Spanish and Mexican periods. Not even the state of welfare dependency that today characterizes much of Hispanic life in northern New Mexico has snuffed out the old fires.

Back in the 1890s, there was a considerable Populist sentiment among Hispanics and some Anglos in Las Vegas. Felix Martinez, a Populist and the editor of *La Voz del Pueblo*, spearheaded the drive in 1892 for building a normal school. After much quarreling between the two halves of Las Vegas, a compromise site for the school was selected, and construction began on New

Mexico Highlands University. A teacher's college that has slowly evolved into a university, the school is a major educational force in northern New Mexico, particularly for Hispanics. Indicative of the financial poverty of much of the state, most of the Highlands students receive some form of federal or state financial assistance in order to remain in school and complete degree programs. Although the architecture of the campus is eclectic, the Spanish Mission style has a strong presence.

Humorous and bizarre cultural cross-currents ripple through the Highlands campus. A few years ago, one student, not noted for his intellectual prowess, was referred to by his classmates as *"el teflón,"* which is Spanish for Teflon. He was called *"el teflón,"* because, as his fellow students said, *"no se le pegaba nada."* That is to say, nothing would stick to him. Another time, a beloved campus security officer stopped a young coed who had run a red light. Siren screaming and red lights flashing, he pulled her car over to the curb.

"Let me see your driver's license," he said in the inimitable accent of a northern New Mexican whose native language is Spanish.

The coed produced her license.

"It says here you need glasses," he said as he glowered at her.

"I've got contacts."

He pulled himself up to his full five feet five inches and said to her in a voice filled with righteous indignation:

"Lady, I don't care who you know." Then he cited her.

During the summer not so long ago, a construction crew on the Highlands University campus excavated a site for a new building. The site happened to be a local cemetery from the last century. Within days, skulls were circulating among the students. A team of anthropologists eventually succeeded in gathering up all the remains and arranging them for a proper inventory and reburial.

There is something peculiarly appropriate about human skulls moving about above the earth in Las Vegas, New Mexico. Here, life and death have been as finely balanced as mountain and plain, Anglo and Hispano, merchant and rancher, lawman and gunslinger, here where Billy the Kid passed through, where Pat Garrett enforced the law and order, here where *Las Gorras Blancas* tore up railroad tracks and turned them into Sherman neckties, here where a boomtown settled into its old ways like a grandfather into his rocking chair, here the skulls of the dead come back to share the incredible landscape, to walk about again before settling down one more time in the earth. Here the dead come back to share the past and the present with the living, to haunt the living who haunt the dead.

"How does it feel, old skeleton, skull bones with matted hair, to walk about again?"

"The wind swirls through my eyes and the holes where my nose used to be, but I feel nothing. I don't even smell the bread fresh from the ovens. Are they still using the ovens?"

"Old skull bones, the ovens burn human flesh in our time."

"Your words cut through me like the cold wind that took me long ago. Is your time the time of hell?"

"It is a time of dreary violence. As was your time. The sunlight comes pouring beautifully through the hole in your head."

"I survived that bullet. Only the years and the cold wind prevailed against me."

"What can you say to me?"

"I have learned the wisdom to smile and say nothing."

"You have no comments for the living?"

"My smile is a comment. My eyes, which you cannot see, are a comment."

"Are you Indio, Chicano, Hispano, Mexicano, or Anglo?"

"I am of an ancient race of starfire, windsong, and clean bone."

"Do you see anything at all? Do you see in color or in black and white?

"I see in the colors of dreams and memory. I see as an object sees staring from a photograph, from the lens of a camera, into the eyes of the living."

"Where does the photograph end, old skull bones, and the image begin, on the printed page or in the mind?"

"When you look at a star, where does your vision end and the star begin?"


## VI

Turning east on National Avenue and facing toward New Town, the Episcopal (left) and Methodist (right) churches rise just off the edge of New Mexico Highlands University. They are a graceful reminder of the simpler and comforting verities from middle America, the Midwest. This quiet and solid middle-class respectability is another facet of Las Vegas society, particularly on the north side of New Town. The Victorian home at Sixth Street and Columbia Avenue is one example, as are the houses on the corner of Sixth Street and Friedman Avenue and along Sixth Street. The home, actually an apartment house, at Eighth Street and Baca Avenue, is known affectionately as Bedpost Manor. The institutional bedposts as well as the decorative lions, grillwork, and fountain, add an unusual stamp of personality to an otherwise nondescript building.

Institutional structures on the north side of New Town, Robertson High School and the Northern New Mexico Rehabilitation Center appear midwestern, as do the fine Victorian houses on Eighth Street. The individualistic touches to these homes show that here the Midwest has reached an extreme extension. The architectural values of turn-of-the-century America begin to frazzle here in the Southwest. The pickup truck disrespectfully parked in the yard of a handsome home speaks of mountain country and more agitated times than the architects dreamed would be in store for these structures.

Interspersed among the finer homes are decaying or dilapidated buildings that still maintain, at times, a highly individuated decorative elegance, as with the ceramic swan beside the home on Fifth Street. Nearby, on Sixth Street and Columbia, is a '50 Buick parked beside a modest two-story home. The '50 Buick, no doubt, joins its brother dream machines from the fifties in their slow-motion parade round and round the plaza and up and down Grand Avenue (U.S. 85).

Wherever there are children, there is usually a mess. Children are ecstatically alive, and life is always messy. The backyard at Sixth Street and Columbia has all the tell-tale signs of active children, or of at least one active child, near the premises. Even the sad signals of distress and poverty, the scattered empty Schlitz beer cans, the grimy back door, the general aura of neglect, are overcome by the toy dump truck, the slide and swing set, the tiny racing car near the fence and the stubborn-looking little plastic horse. This backyard, with its infinite possibilities for make-believe worlds, is a paradise for any young child.

Although it has seen better days, the house at the corner of Sixth Street and Columbia carries its faded elegance with grace. The paint is chipped on the charming porch, the fenced-in yard overgrown with weeds and indifference, and the "for sale" sign faces a quiet street. The sense of absence is, at times, overpowering in Las Vegas.

It is possible to look at the Victorian stick-style home on Eighth Street and forget that this is the late twentieth century. Suddenly it is 1917. Excited voices ring out inside the house. A young girl laughs as she runs down the stairs with her boyfriend in hot pursuit. "Be careful," her mother shouts in a friendly warm sing-song. There is a patriotic rally that afternoon. The Anglos and the Hispanos affirm that they are one people. It is time to shed someone else's blood. On July 20, José Cisneros is the first

prospective draftee whose number is drawn. Hurrahs and cheers. It is over in a year, and twelve coffins return to Las Vegas from World War I. The young girl walks stiffly down the stairs for the next forty years, every morning, on her way to teach at a local grade school.

## VII

The veneer of substance and prosperity can be maintained only so long in Las Vegas. A city that has suffered so many economic problems for so much of its history carries not only the obvious scars of poverty but also the imprints left by desperate hands clinging to the lowest rungs of the economic ladder. For a few, the gleaming aluminum trailer may be a sign of affluence, especially when it is parked next to the new brick home. For others, however, the modest house is a small step up from the trailer, the run-down adobe, or the creaking and weathered Victorian house. For many, the mobile home, as the one in Uppertown, is as tentative in its rise out of poverty as the first amphibian that crawls out of the primeval sea. The low-cost housing on Hot Springs Boulevard also looks more like a hope rather than a secure reality that abject poverty is a thing of the past. The same may be said for the trailers along Route 3. They have the appearance of updated prairie schooners that made it this far, to the outskirts of town, and then petrified to become one with the earth. They stretch out along the highway. No need to form a circle against marauders. This time the marauders are not the Indians but rather low-income, insufficient education, and the limited opportunities here on the edge of the limitless plains. The new marauders have won all the skirmishes and have settled in to stay for a long time. If the day is long beneath the lowering sky, there is always K Mart and the promise of a meager cornucopia from the American Dream. For those who hunger, there are the predictable fast-food chains and the hamburger stands.

Forsaking the dream of a home in favor of a trailer is the kind of compromise more and more people have been forced to make in our times. Trailers come in models, like new cars, and for a brief period, they have a manufactured, mass produced quality of newness. The trailers along Route 3 have a smart appearance about them, yet altogether jarring against the plains and the bare hills. Two time frames, one ancient, primeval, and the other up-to-date, totally contemporary, meet and coexist here. The photographer has caught his own shadow in the picture and has thereby created an allusion to yet other time frames. The shadow resembles a vanished unicorn able to exist now only on the edges of things, on the margins of trailer parks, in the recesses of imagination, on the outskirts of town. The shadow could also be the image of Don Quijote de La Mancha setting out one more time to right the wrongs of the world. He has paused here, at the edge of this new reality called a trailer park, to study it, to contemplate the town beyond and the vast plains that are very much like the plains of La Mancha, to find, no doubt, that there are more wrongs ever to be set right. Don Quijote would bring to these sons and daughters of Hispanos and pioneers, and Indians, railroad workers, and ranchers, merchants, and outlaws, a vision of social justice and harmony, good government, and, above all, a vision of insanity combined with method, which is what we call genius.

Or is this shadow only a dark rider heralding a bleak future about to come around the bend in the road? There is a slight suggestion here, also, of *la huesuda*, Death, who is sometimes called the bony-faced woman, *la Sebastiana*, waiting at the edge of the trailer park, ready to take someone away from here forever, perhaps someone from the house near the dumpster.

The battered shell of the old Chevy pickup truck near a trailer and a house recalls the harshness of the 1920s and the Great Depression. Long before then, however, there had been hard times dating back to the "Bust of

'93." For the Hispanos, poverty was deeply rooted in the old system of land peonage, in the lack of English language skills, in the lack of technical skills suitable to an increasingly urban-oriented society. While under the New American dispensation, there was an attempt to provide equal protection under the law, the right to vote, and the right to a free public education; there was no concerted attempt to provide the economic, social, and educational structures, programs, and institutions to facilitate the transition for the Hispanos from an agrarian, precapitalistic, communal mode of existence to the industrial, economically competitive, and privatized style of the English-speaking nation. Indeed, the provision of such structures would have been anathema to the laissez-faire ideology of that time.

The 1920s didn't start out on a sour note. World War I was over, the loss in lives had been slight in Las Vegas, and there was hope that new enterprises would revive the town. The Storrie Lake project, designed to build a dam on the Gallinas north of Las Vegas, had the promise of bringing agricultural prosperity. The automobile and the airplane promised recreational development of the area. Even the movie business seemed a promise on the horizon. As early as 1913, Romaine Fielding, an early star of the silent films, came to Las Vegas with the Lubin Company to produce such films as *The Rattlesnake, Evil Eye,* and *Where Mountain and Valley Meet.* Fielding wrote and produced a "five-reel thriller" called the *Golden God,* depicting labor uprisings against industrial monopolies. The Old Town plaza and the Plaza Hotel were the locales for this epic. Then in 1915, Tom Mix, a friend of Charles Ilfeld, came to town and, in fact, began his career here, making his first movie called *Never Again.* Tom Mix also made the first two of his cowboy classics here, *The Rancher's Daughter* and *The Country Drugstore.*

These promising beginnings soon fizzled. Ambrose Bierce's definition of an "opportunity" as a "favorable occasion for grasping a disappointment" would seem to apply to Las Vegas. Agriculture remained in the doldrums, despite work on the Storrie Lake project. The drought of 1934 virtually dried up the Gallinas River. Some growth occurred around the auto-servicing business, but no major airport located here. The movie business went elsewhere. The town, in a sense, never recovered from the "Bust of '93" that effectively ended the boom years throughout the West.

The hard times of the 1920s became horrendously worse with the Great Depression. By the early 1930s, the small tourist trade had disappeared. In 1932, the city of Las Vegas was unable to pay its bills, and the county and state governments had overdrawn their funds. The private relief organizations were overwhelmed with the numbers of suffering people seeking relief. During the worst days of the Great Depression, Las Vegas, like many other American communities, made the city jail available with free meals and lodging for transients.

Many of the houses in Las Vegas still have a depression aura about them. The mud-spattered car parked in front of the tin-roofed house recalls that earlier era. Even the restoration effort made for the old Ford cars out on Highway 85 brings back the time when things as they were had to make do with a little paint and bailing wire because there was no money available to replace them.

Two institutions in American society bear a remarkable resemblance to one another—the university and the mental hospital. Both promise a better life for their clientele and, for the most part, fail to live up to that promise. Las Vegas is singularly blessed with having both institutions, New Mexico Highlands University and the New Mexico State Hospital. Both have lovely campuses, and both offer programs for human growth and development. The hulking State Hospital Administration Building, with its somber Romanesque arch, could as well serve as the administrative center for a university.

Once a visitor to the state hospital took a

wrong turn and passed by the ward for the elderly. He heard a piano tune coming from the room and saw a nurse dressed in white keeping time to the music, clapping her hands and thump, thumping her foot. Seated around another nurse, who played the tune on an ancient Baldwin, some on the floor, some in chairs, and a few in wheelchairs, the white-wisped and bald heads of these ancient patients swayed back and forth, back and forth, as they sang in choir:

*Oh we ain't got a barrel of money,*
*maybe we're ragged and funny,*
*but we'll travel along, singing our song,*
*side by side.*

The visitor quicky left.

## VIII

The sun rises, sets, rises again, or rather the earth continues its measured pace around the sun. Throughout the universe, there is the dance of particles, the balance of forces, cataclysmic deaths, and rebirths of galaxies scattered over unimaginable reaches of space and time. For unknown wishes, dreams, desires, or reasons, or for no good reason at all, discrete bundles of energy, highly unstable and empty space for the most part, hold together in human form for a few years on this planet, then break down into more stable forms of "matter," whatever that is or may turn out to be. While they live, they live restless lives; uncomfortable bipeds they are, who must find something to do every moment of their existence. Las Vegas is a kind of living museum, an ongoing street theater of the tragicomic dimensions of the human condition. Against a backdrop of the awesome mountains and the vast, haunting plains, the humans who have chosen, or been chosen by birth or circum-stances, to live here fling up their earth adobe houses and rubblestone buildings as sets for them to act out their brief parts in this local drama.

Generations come and go. The old sets, adobe, rubblestone, and wood, well preserved in this arid land, outlast their temporary inhabitants. People are born, walk about, and are laid to rest, while all around them in Las Vegas are the artifacts, the monuments they have wrought with their own hands. The Fort Union Drive-In Theater on Route 3 looks ever so much like a cemetery. The blank screen speaks with pitiless honesty about the meaning or knowledge of meaning that we have of all these lives gathered here and elsewhere on the planet. The speaker posts, to continue the analogy, are the grave markers for last year's cars and their passengers and their ancestors before them, turned now to bone, to ash, to fresh loam for next spring's growth of green on the earth, turned now to rusted husks of steel, the paint faded, chipped, or gone, the headlights gone and empty eye sockets left behind.

Somehow, the reassurance of certified premium quality on the falling-apart billboard advertisement for beer does not reassure anyone that this lonely, empty space will fill up with anything that has human meaning.

Yet, it is precisely in the empty space that men and women have built up the meanings of their own existence. The dog in front of the church near Montezuma, above and to the west of Las Vegas, is a reminder of the human presence. The mural art on the church marks one attempt to fill the empty space with light, with warmth. Another church near the skating pond, also in Montezuma, is, for all practical purposes, identical to the churches that have stood in northern New Mexico for centuries. The old Pueblo style has been transformed into the Territorial with the white-trimmed windows and the pitched tin roof, but the basic symbol of the church remains unchanged. It speaks of faith that the empty space, somehow, is not really empty.

For horses and other animals, there is no empty space. The six horses gathered on the snowy plains east of town are resplendent in their winter coats. They fill out the plentitude

51

of their lives moment by moment, season by season, until they die or are destroyed:

*Black horses*
*Light horse*
*Pinto in a snowy field*

*Winter horses*
*No rider will know you*
*As you are now*

*Six horses standing in snow*
*Forever now in memory*
*Near a fence and a road*

*Horses for a cold landscape*
*You stand now*
*Proud in your shaggy finery*

*Cold sentinels of dreams*
*You stand guard*
*Over all winter fields*

*Horses near Las Vegas*
*You stand immobile as stone*
*Six icons carved by light*

A dog crosses the fields northeast of Las Vegas. Lonely the landscape and lonely the history of this town in recent years.

The Great Depression was followed by World War II. Just prior to the beginning of that conflict, the 200th and 515th Coast Artillery units of the New Mexico National Guard were sent to the Philippines. Most of the men of these units had trained at Camp Luna on the outskirts of Las Vegas. They were sent to the Philippines primarily because they spoke Spanish. Not long after Pearl Harbor, these troops were captured, tortured at Bataan and in the infamous Death March. Many died, and the lives of the survivors were severely shortened as a result of the treatment they received at the hands of their captors. Those who returned found a small town that grew but slowly. The

principal sources of income were and have remained employment in federal, state, county, or local government, employment in federal or state heavily subsidized institutions such as New Mexico Highlands University or the state hospital, and the Camp Luna facilities. Ranching and service industries also provide some employment.

For over a century, from the time of the founding of Las Vegas by Juan de Dios Maese in 1835 until the present, a continual parade of lives has passed through these meadows. For the most part, they have been the good people of this earth, the people of whom the Spanish poet Antonio Machado spoke when he said:

> *And everywhere I have seen*
> *people who dance or play,*
> *whenever they can, and they work*
> *their small piece of land.*
> *Never, if they arrive some place,*
> *do they ask where they are.*
> *When they travel, they ride*
> *on the back of an old mule,*
> *and they never hurry,*
> *not even on feast days.*
> *Where there is wine, they drink wine;*
> *Where there is no wine, fresh water.*
> *They are good people who live,*
> *work, pass by and dream,*
> *and on a day like any other,*
> *they rest beneath the earth.**

They have tasted of the wine when there was wine and of water when there was only water, and have gone their way like all men. They have left behind in Las Vegas the varied monuments to themselves, to their belief in the endurance of what they valued, of what their very lives meant. If their dreams were built upon illusions, so are the dreams of all people. The town, finally, remains.

*Antonio Machado, "Soledades, II," *Obras Completas* (Madrid, 1977). The translation is by the author.

54

Population trends have been negative in recent years. Hispanics have lost some communal lands in the surrounding countryside; the villages have suffered depopulation; and the youth of the area have been moving away for lucrative employment elsewhere.

Not so long ago, in 1955, Ramon Maes, the grandson of Juan de Dios Maese, first alcalde of Las Vegas, described the loss of access to grazing lands in his nearby village and lamented that without water the community could not grow. Yet Las Vegas lives. The United World College campus at the old Montezuma Hotel (one of the nineteenth-century relics) has once again raised hopes that prosperity may return. Above all, the meadows, the plains, and the mountains remain.

The house and the pond at the edge of the eastern plains are the two poles between which the drama has been played out here, man and nature, frail structures upon the timeless earth, the fast-decay timeclocks built into humans and into all things human versus the slowly evolving changes of nature, the rapid pace of daily existence versus the millennial voyage of the planet across the galaxy. Cars speed by on Interstate 25 and on old U.S. 85. Off to the side of the road, on the high ground of the plains, are the ruts, clearly visible, left by the Conestoga wagons, the prairie schooners of the Santa Fe Trail. High above, a north-bound jet leaves contrails in the sky.

Nature keeps its own counsel. The grasses growing beside the pond give the small body of water the appearance of an eye, as if nature had chosen this spot to look up at the overarching sky and reflect back the eternal drift of clouds. There abides, finally, the gamble of nature. So much of the world remains, at least to the human eye, insensate. This is a deception. New life constantly pushes up from loam, from darkness, the new life emerging into and merging with the onrushing future.

A close-up photograph of grasses reveals their hypnotic power. These grasses beckon one to come to them, to explore them, to part the life-giving and life-protecting strands, to seek there a communion, an abandonment, the ultimate pleasure of affirming life against the nihilism of silence and nothingness. There is messiness here. Life is messy in its conception, in its development, in its crises, and in its stirrings to renew itself. It is a kind of wild dance. Las Vegas, as a community, has learned to do that dance, to dance with death in its own streets, to make a fiesta of failure, to scale the bones of its own past, to swirl on in the dance with all the other dancers, and continue the dance to the end, to the very end, even when the steps in the dance are most uncertain, to dance on and on, to enjoy it, and to muddle through somehow. That is all we have the right to hope for, whether it be an individual or a community, that the dance go on, that it be enjoyed, and that it be gotten through somehow.

E. A. MARES

# LAS VEGAS, NEW MEXICO

Old Town Plaza, North Side

Old Town Plaza, Facing Northeast

Old Town Plaza, Facing East

Facing South Pacific Avenue from Side Street

Adobe Houses, South Pacific Avenue

Portale, South Pacific Avenue

House, Hot Springs Boulevard

71

4:30 Amtrak Train

Train Station and Atchison, Topeka & Santa Fe Boxcar

Boxcar and Warehouse Building

Boxcars and Houses

Baggage Cart, Train Station

Roundhouse

Casino Bar, Railroad and Lincoln Avenues

85

Facing North on Lincoln Avenue

Masonic Building and El Fidel Hotel, from Grand Avenue

Tony's Food Market, Lincoln Avenue

Buildings, Eleventh Street

House, Jackson Avenue at Tenth Street

95

New Mexico Jaycees Parade Car, Tenth Street

Corner of Jackson and Tenth Streets

Between Sixth and Seventh Streets

Murphey's Drug Store, Douglas Avenue

'58 Ford in Front of J. C. Penney's, Douglas Avenue

Corner of Douglas Avenue and Sixth Street

J. C. Penney's Window, Douglas Avenue

'55 Buick, Old Safeway Parking Lot on Douglas Avenue

111

City Schools Building, Armory, Bus Depot, and Post Office, Douglas Avenue

Bridge Street, Facing West Toward Old Town Plaza

Ilfeld Auditorium, Highlands University Campus

Episcopal (l.) and Methodist (r.) Churches, Facing East on National Avenue

119

Victorian Home, Sixth Street and Columbia Avenue

Corner of Sixth Street and Friedman Avenue

Houses, Sixth Street

Home (Bedpost Manor), Eighth Street and Baca Avenue

Robertson High School, Fifth Street and Friedman Avenue

Northern New Mexico Rehabilitation Center, Eighth Street and Friedman Avenue

Houses, Eighth Street

Pickup Truck and House, Eighth Street

135

Victorian House and Ceramic Swan, Fifth Street

Houses and '50 Buick, Fifth Street

House, Corner of Sixth Street and Columbia Avenue

House, Eighth Street Extension

House and Trailer, Eighth Street Extension

Homes, Subdivision at Edge of Eastern Plains

Low Cost Housing, Hot Springs Boulevard

K-Mart, Route 3

151

Facing North, Grand Avenue (I-25 Extension)

153

Blake's Lotaburger, Route 3

Tim Romero's Trailer Park, Route 3

157

Truck, Homes, Uppertown

Old Ford Cars, Highway 85

Administration Building at State Hospital, Hot Springs Boulevard

Facing West on Plains near Route 3

Fort Union Drive-In Theatre, Route 3

Dog in Front of Church with Mural, Montezuma

Church near Skating Pond, Montezuma

Horses, Winter, Plains East of Town

Becca, Fields Northeast of Town

House and Pond at Edge of Eastern Plains

Grasses and Pond, East of Route 3

Grasses

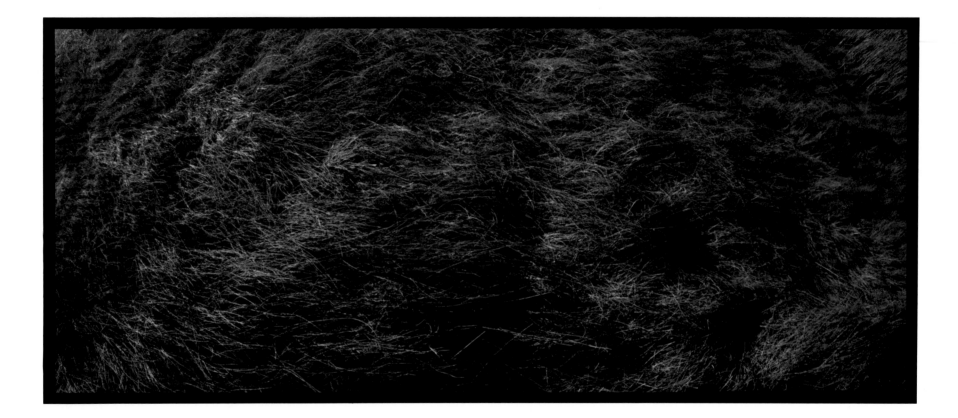

181

LAS VEGAS, NEW MEXICO
was designed by Emmy Ezzell,
with type composed by the
University of New Mexico Printing Plant
in Merganthaler Linotron Trump Medieval,
and manufactured by
the Christian Board of Publication.
It is printed on Warren's Lustro Cream paper,
and bound in Holliston Roxite cloth.